D0821828

ADVANCE PRAISE FOR

## RABBIT AT THE SLIDING DOOR

"Denise Lee Branco creates a masterful story about the animal and human bond filled with inspiration, humor, and love. Share the special journey of a small happenstance visitor who thumped her way into the author's heart and life."

-Valerie Ormond
**Multiple-Award Winning Author of**
**The *Believing in Horses* series**

"*Rabbit at the Sliding Door* is as heartwarming a tale as *The Velveteen Rabbit*, but Chloe's Story takes readers on a true and inspiring adventure the whole way through. A treasure of love between Denise and the bunny who "found" her, this is a story of hope, needed in our troubling times."

-June Gillam
**Author of *So Sweet Against Your Teeth,***
***Poems of Childhood's Fall***

"I can't think of a more beautiful way to spend an afternoon than to read about Chloe—how a chance meeting brings a new friend into our lives and makes a lifelong impression that stays with us forever. Writing about our beloved pets is challenging, but Denise Lee Branco does it masterfully. I wanted to pet Chloe's ears, stroke her tail, and pull her into my lap to snuggle. We're right with you, Denise, feeling love from you and our new little friend. Thank you for taking us through the ups and downs of life. While we usually outlive our pets, grief in time turns into gratitude. Glad you were there for Chloe. She knew exactly who to find. In finding you, she found all of us."

-Kimberly A. Edwards, President
**California Writers Club Sacramento**

"When I settle down with a cup of coffee and an unopened book, the possibilities are endless. Love, intrigue, adventure, conflict, mystery, inspiration...just waiting to unfold. *Rabbit at the Sliding Door: Chloe's Story* by Denise Lee Branco, award-winning author and inspirational speaker, was today's delightful page-turner, filled with all the elements necessary for an afternoon well spent. First page to the last, Ms. Branco did an excellent job of capturing the beauty of an unusual love between a mysterious palomino rabbit named Chloe, and a tender-hearted young woman who would show Chloe unconditional love and devotion from the first day they met. Animal lovers of all ages will enjoy this sweet inspirational story."

**-Pat Wright**
**Poet and Storyteller**

"Every story or book that this author pens, she writes from her heart. Anyone who reads her work, will be captivated by her writing."

**-Dottie Doss, Avid Reader**

"Denise Lee Branco in *Rabbit at the Sliding Door*, writes a captivating, true story of befriending an abandoned rabbit that has gone somewhat wild, and how this rabbit becomes her precious Chloe and enriches her life. Throughout the pages readers can delight in the charm of the life of a rabbit and also the dear contemplations of the author as she seeks to be a dedicated pet owner. Denise Lee Branco's love for animals shows through beautifully."

**-Heidi Vertrees**
**Royal Dragonfly Award-Winning Author of**
***Victor Survives Being a Kid* and Educator**

"This story is charming and informative. I hadn't realized how much I didn't know about rabbits until I read Denise's book. I thoroughly enjoyed it."

**-P. L. Clark**
**Western Author of *William's Quest***

"*Rabbit at the Sliding Door* is an enduring story that is sure to put a smile on your face and remind you of God's good gifts. Denise Lee Branco helps us to see how important animals are to our lives. She reminds us that we have the responsibility of being good stewards of these special friends. Branco said, "I needed Chloe, and she needed me." God meets us in our moments of need with sweet opportunities that take us on a journey of healing and delight. This personal story of love, loss, and hope will be enjoyed by readers of all ages and remind us of our responsibility of taking care of God's creation."

-Tim Riordan
Pastor of SonRise Baptist Church in Newnan, GA,
and Author of numerous books including
*Songs from the Heart: Meeting with God in the Psalms*

"What a lovely story! Denise brings you into her world of compassion and abiding love for a simple, lost creature who finds a safe, comfortable home. This book belongs on the shelf next to *Black Beauty* as another exemplary tale of love and kindness for our animal friends."

-Beth Bridges
The Networking Motivator/Author and Speaker

"I thoroughly enjoyed reading *Rabbit at the Sliding Door*. This sweet story made me more aware of the different types of animals that may need to be rescued. If you are an animal lover, like me, this is the story for you."

-Susan U. Neal RN, MBA, MHS
Author of *Eat God's Food*

"If you're a true animal lover, then *Rabbit at the Sliding Door* is a must-read. I literally laughed and cried while reading this delightful tale of Chloe's adventures."

-**Dana Cotta**
**Lifelong Animal Lover**

"The book *Rabbit at the Sliding Door: Chloe's Story* by Denise Lee Branco is a delight to read. I fell in love with Chloe and enjoyed reading about her adventures. This book also taught me about the life of rabbits and why they deserve our protection. I recommend it to anyone who likes animal stories."

-**Sandra D. Simmer**
**NCPA Published Author and Poet**

"This is a heartwarming tale about when a compassionate person meets an animal in need. Everyone could glean something from this story about life, love and the importance of the human-animal bond."

-**Alex Rensing, DVM**

"They say that good things come in small packages, which is a perfect description for this book. Readers won't be able to resist bonding with the well-developed characters, including Chloe the rabbit. The plot is full of surprises, since Chloe is not your average rabbit, and the main character comes up with ideas and solutions that honor and celebrate Chloe's needs and personality rather than the human's convenience. The emotional connection between these two rings true on every page and will touch readers, reminding them of animals they've loved. In summation, this is a lovely, well-written book that I am happy to recommend."

-**Sharon S. Darrow**
**Author and Publisher**

# Rabbit

## at the
# Sliding Door

Chloe's Story

Copyright 2022 by Denise Lee Branco

Website: www.deniseinspiresyou.com
Twitter & Instagram: @deniseleebranco
Facebook: DeniseInspiresYou
LinkedIn: denise-lee-branco-27309824/

All rights reserved. No part of this publication may be reproduced, stored in retrieval system, or transmitted in any form or by any means—electronic, mechanical, recording, photocopy, scanning or otherwise—except for brief quotations in critical articles and reviews, without the prior permission of the author.

Limit of Liability/Disclaimer of Warranty: While the publisher and author have used their best efforts in preparing this book, they make no representations or warranties with respect to the accuracy or completeness of the contents of this book and specifically disclaim any implied warranties of merchantability or fitness for a particular purpose. No warranty may be created or extended by sales representatives or written sales materials. The advice and strategies contained herein may not be suitable for your situation. You should consult with a professional when appropriate. Neither the publisher nor the author shall be liable for any loss of profit or any other commercial damages, including but not limited to special, incidental, consequential, personal or other damages.

All internet addresses, phone numbers, company or product information, etc. in this book are offered as a resource. They are not intended in any way to be or imply an endorsement by the author or publisher, nor does the author or publisher vouch for the content of these resources for the life of this book.

*Rabbit at the Sliding Door: Chloe's Story*

Published by Strolling Hills Publishing, LLC
P.O. Box 674
Lincoln, CA 95648

Book cover/interior/eBook design by the Book Cover Whisperer:
OpenBookDesign.biz

Library of Congress Control Number: 2022903800

PET011000    PETS / Rabbits, Mice, Hamsters, Guinea Pigs, etc.

REL012040    RELIGION / Christian Living / Inspirational

BIO026000    BIOGRAPHY & AUTOBIOGRAPHY / Personal Memoirs

978-0-9845888-2-4 Hardcover
978-0-9845888-3-1 eBook


FIRST EDITION

# Rabbit

## at the

## Sliding Door

## Chloe's Story

### Denise Lee Branco

*Strolling Hills Publishing*

This book is dedicated to my precious Chloe,
and other abandoned pet rabbits,
because every bunny deserves a
loving family and paradise on Earth.

# CONTENTS

# INTRODUCTION

God entrusts us to protect and provide for His crea-
tures with love and respect. We are His animal
caretakers here on Earth, and we should consider it a
great privilege to be blessed with that duty. I believe
they are divinely sent to us at the precise moment we
need them, whether we know it or not.

I can't imagine going through every decade of my
life without an animal companion. They have brought
me endless joy, love and laughter, and taught life lessons
I didn't know I needed. I am better because of every
furry or feathered friend who graced my life.

It feels like I could never repay them for all they've
done for me, but I can try by telling their stories and
sharing the beauty of our human/animal bond. I'd
like you to meet a special bunny who greeted me at

my sliding door one summer morning and leaped into my heart forever.

My hope is that Chloe's story will encourage pet adoption—not as an irresponsible impulse decision, but one with lifelong certainty into a permanent home (or in Chloe's case, a rabbit sanctuary). My prayer is that there will come a day when no animal experiences abandonment or abuse, but instead receives the everlasting unconditional love they deserve.

My wish is that you will feel you're right there with Chloe and me, living life to the fullest, as you hop along with us on the pages of this book.

# DOUBLE-TAKE

Walking out the side door of the garage to a combination of gravel-road mix, topsoil, and unwanted weeds always reminded this single woman of her lack of money to even install a basic concrete walkway. And yet I liked it that way. Having a natural, rural feel to the landscape reminded me of my country-living upbringing.

I planted a variety of flowers, shrubbery, and small trees around the perimeter of my yard and set granite stepping stones from the redwood deck to the unfinished side yard along the edge of the sod. My father and I built the redwood deck that bumped up to the glass sliding window of my house. In one corner of my garden, a concrete water fountain stood, with water cascading over an umbrella held by a boy, girl, and their puppy.

With winters in mind, I'd created a make-shift moat that would move water from the backyard to the front when the volume of heavy downpours were more than what the ground drain could handle. My simple solution: shoveling a mini ditch under the fence gate so water could travel out to the street and into the city drain. It may have looked odd—the only yard in the neighborhood with a three-inch gap of light under its solid wood gate—but hey, it worked.

✦ ✦ ✦

MONDAY BEGAN WITH THE clock alarm on my nightstand buzzing at 5:30 a.m. It seemed like the first weekend in June 2011 couldn't possibly be over, but that morning's wake-up call reminded me that it was. I headed straight to my sliding glass door in the kitchen to allow early morning summer air to flow through the screen door. I pulled items from my refrigerator and packed my lunch, took a shower, put on makeup, and got dressed. Once my normal routine was finished and I was ready to leave for work, I headed back to the kitchen, dragged the slider to its closed position with one hand while simultaneously reaching for my insulated lunch box with the other. *Ohhhhhh…wait a minute. What was that?*

Out of the corner of my eye, I caught a visitor sitting on the redwood deck at the screen door. I never would have guessed that a rabbit—and a young one at that—would be sitting in my fenced-in suburban backyard, but there she was. In her youthful, energetic way, she hopped over to a nearby purple petunia plant and began nibbling at the perennial, hinting as to her morning hunger. I wasn't positive whether she was a cottontail or domesticated rabbit based on her small size and coloring.

It was time to leave for work, but my new friend seemed unfulfilled with the petunia plant as she hopped back to the screen and stared at me. I sensed she wasn't wild, because I could see that she wanted to come inside my house when I opened the screen door. Perhaps she saw my two indoor cats peering back at her with extreme interest and was drawn to them; or sadly, she belonged to someone and was used to living indoors. Nevertheless, I couldn't let her inside and leave her unsupervised with my cats or even in an unfamiliar room by herself while I was gone for the day.

Flashbacks to my youth raising rabbits for my 4-H project surfaced and I started thinking about what else I could feed her. I rummaged through my refrigerator and found enough iceberg lettuce to hopefully satisfy my new guest for that morning until I could buy more rabbit-appropriate food later.

I left for work and wondered if my morning visitor would be there when I returned home. Would she come back the next day? How did she even get there in the first place, and all the way to the back of my house? She must have come through that gap under the gate. It had to be those three inches of light under the gate that beckoned her with curiosity.

## PALOMINO ANGEL

There was no "lost pet" bulletin posted on mailbox units around the neighborhood. Was the rabbit lost? Or had she been dumped, left behind to fend for herself?

She arrived early summer, and from my past experience raising rabbits in my teens, her smaller size suggested she was three to four months old. Counting back a few months, she could have quite possibly been a no-longer-wanted Easter gift. Or had she fallen victim to the decline of home values and the rise of neighborhood foreclosures?

I couldn't bring myself to conclude that this sweet, adorable bunny was dropped off on the side of the road. How could someone be that heartless? Maybe her human family was distraught, unable to even take care of themselves as they dealt with job loss and a no-longer-affordable home mortgage? Foreclosures were happening all over the country.

My subdivision bordered open space—native grasses, oak trees, and creeks—where jack rabbits and cottontails dwelled. Perhaps her owner believed that releasing a rabbit into an environment like that, among other rabbits, would be a more natural way to live.

During the first few days of the rabbit's backyard visits, I named her *Petunia* after she had devoured all my potted petunias, but that name didn't sit well with me. Then, it hit me. Chloe! It would be short for *fore"Chloe"sure* bunny. Even if I never found out if she truly was a doe (female rabbit), or whether she was a foreclosure victim or an unwanted Easter present, the name "Chloe" felt much more cheerful in light of her homeless situation.

Why did Chloe choose my home? What caused her to pick my fence to hop under when she had no clue what was in store for her on the other side? Was she an animal angel sent here to enrich my life?

My beloved horse, Freedom, had passed away three years before. We had a deep bond, and I missed him so. After his death, I looked for another horse to buy, but soon realized that no horse could replace the love I still have for Freedom. Every great story has an ending, and I came to terms with the fact that he may indeed be my last horse.

After some research, I learned that Chloe was domesticated, and her golden coat and size meant that she was a Palomino rabbit. Horses and rabbits eat much of the same types of food—greens, hay, and carrots. *Okay, God. You sure have a sense of humor to send me this type of Palomino after I said that I'd probably never have another horse, but I'm glad you did. She's so cute, and I'm already terribly attached to her. She makes my days much brighter. Thank you, Lord, for showing her the way to me.*

## OPEN RANGE

For about four months, Chloe roamed suburbia. I lived on a circular street and most of the time, I'd see her within a block's distance. I found myself searching the terrain for her when I rode my bike or drove down the street and discovered where her favorite places to dwell were in the neighborhood.

I'd often see her lying on the dirt under a shrub by the front patio of a home four houses away. Most times, she'd be in my front yard or both of my next-door neighbors' yards. She'd often be spread out under a parked car, enjoying moments of leisure. While she looked content, without a care in the world, I was constantly concerned for her safety.

When I'd see her bolt across the street to my other neighbor's property to eat grass or hang out in their flowerbeds, I panicked. She probably did the same thing when I wasn't around, and that realization caused me to worry all the time about her getting hit by a car or attacked by raptors or a dog off leash.

Once, I didn't see Chloe in the neighborhood for more than 24 hours. I got in my car and coasted down my circular street in search of her. Around the bend, I found Chloe eating grass in a front yard. I still remember my sinking feeling, "That's too far away, Chloe! Oh, please come home!"

She returned the following day to the complimentary variety of food that always awaited her on my redwood deck. It brought me immense joy to watch her darling white teeth crunch the delectable offering before her and then hop over to her water bowl afterwards and see her sweet little mouth lap water. I will always treasure those endearing moments.

Like me, my two indoor cats were thrilled to see her. Chloe frequently came to the slider screen when she saw them sitting there, and they'd all touch noses through the mesh. They were the only animal friends she had, and it was endearing to witness their affection.

I wished I hadn't convinced myself that it was best for Chloe to roam free for those many months; that she'd feel confined otherwise. If only I had given her permanent safety on my property when she first came

to my house. That delay came close to being a trag-
ic mistake.

## EVIL RUSE

The animal trap was a red flag for me—a sickening feeling in the pit of my stomach. Its shape, its intricate wiring—part cage/part mechanism—did not need an explanatory label. I didn't know if it was a kill trap or a humane one, but I knew what it signified. Once or twice my parents had to borrow a similar looking cage from the pound back on the ranch where I grew up—a rural necessity to protect our cattle from predatory wildlife.

How could my neighbor, the owner of a rowdy Scottish Terrier, want to trap a defenseless rabbit? I couldn't believe he would do something like that to my Chloe. In recent days, I had noticed Chloe a time or two nibbling out of a small bowl set just inside his garage when the garage door was opened. It all made perfect sense. His intention was not of compassion to feed a lonesome, stray rabbit. He was baiting her!

*I'm stunned. This can't be happening. You mean it's down to this? Chloe's life is literally at stake? What am I going to do?* The only alternative I had was to find out whether my fears had any truth to them and to knock on the door of my neighbor's house.

His wife answered the door. I asked her if they were trying to trap the rabbit, because I'd been caring for it in my backyard for months. She replied vaguely, saying something about how she didn't know anything about "those animals," implying that she was unfamiliar with rabbits but never actually uttering the word *rabbit*. She beckoned her husband to the front door and he stepped outside. He seemed evasive, never quite giving me a straight answer. I asked him for one night—just one night of time to block Chloe in my backyard so that I could keep her off the street and care for her.

You'd think that would be the solution to his problem. He began to complain about Chloe eating the plants in his garden. He said, "Good Luck," adding that he hadn't had any success catching her thus far. I felt intense worry for Chloe as well as pride that she could outsmart that horrible man. Way to go, Chloe!

I asked again if he would give me until morning to

block Chloe in my yard. I could feel a mother's instinct arise in me as there was no way I was going to let him harm Chloe. No way! It seemed like this situation became more of a competition with him in that moment. The better man (or woman) would win. Their neighborly friendliness had waned in time and become a bit forced; and here was another situation where it felt that he had no intention of being nice to me or showing kindness towards a rabbit who wouldn't hurt anyone.

And then, he uttered words that I will NEVER forget. Obviously fed up with my persistence, he proclaims that Chloe was fair game: "whoever caught her, would keep her." I stood there motionless in sheer drop-your-jaw shock as I watched him storm away. What was he planning to do with her? Make rabbit stew?

Anger, worry, frustration, panic—they all set in, but all I could do was pray. Pray that Chloe would choose to return to my backyard that night. Faith was my answer. There was no way I could sleep that night knowing that danger lurked next door.

✦ ✦ ✦

FIRST ITEM OF BUSINESS for my rabbit stakeout was to open the sliding glass to expose the screen door so I could hear even the slightest crunching from Chloe. My senses were heightened that night. Crickets serenaded while dogs barked. A slight summer breeze rustled through a nearby Japanese maple tree.

The one and only way in and out of my fenced-in backyard for an independent traveler like Chloe was the three-inch gap under a locked, solid wood gate. She knew the route well. Chloe usually came home for dinner and left in the morning. She'd squeeze under the gate, hop up the gravel-mix side yard, turn down the aggregate stepping stone path, and go up the step to my redwood deck where a meal, water, and a dry bed of straw awaited her.

In true Cinderella-like fashion, making it home thirty minutes before the clock struck midnight, Chloe hopped up on my redwood deck and started nibbling away at an even larger assortment of fine cuisine arranged for her under the picnic table. *Yay, Chloe's here!*

I grabbed items from my garage and lying around the yard to block her exit at the gate—paint cans, bricks, plywood, large stones, etc.—and headed out to create a permanent barrier to the world Chloe once knew. A new chapter in her life was about to unfold— one safe from harm. Thank God, Chloe was finally protected for the rest of her days.

She was home to stay. Or was she?

## THE GREAT ESCAPE

Hallelujah! I saved Chloe from a scavenging, dangerous life on the streets. She was free from mean people, car wheels, birds of prey, and chasing dogs. I was relieved and at peace. I could finally sleep well knowing that I would never have to worry about Chloe losing her life ever again.

Well, that's what I thought until the moment when my heart sank once more—the instant I saw the gap of light reappear at another section of my solid wood fence. This time in dirt in the corner between the wall of the house and the fence post which held up the gate, big enough for a rabbit to shimmy through.

Tears began to flow. My dear Chloe was gone! How in the world was I so clueless to not see an area of softer dirt where Chloe could dig out? Here I was trying to protect her, and she was so scared about being cut off from a life of freedom that she bolted. Why would she even want to roam free when she had a continuous buffet of delectable cuisine at my house?

That darn animal trap! Oh, I hoped Chloe made it past that stupid contraption. Or did he capture her this time? Did he win his self-proclaimed game of catch? Frantic, I made my rounds through the neighborhood, searching those areas I knew she frequented. No sign of Chloe.

I was about to accept the fact that I had a lost pet when one more idea came to mind. There was a slim chance that someone took her to my local SPCA. Trying to observe the rules of the road, but at the same time, hoping to get there as quickly as possible, I headed to the shelter. Time was of the essence.

At the SPCA, I shared my story with as many volunteers as I could. I asked, "Did someone bring in a golden-colored rabbit?" "No" was the repeated response, but I was invited to stroll the "available critters" section of the shelter. I looked in every cage but no Chloe.

I slumped back into my car, discouraged and blue. On the drive home, my eyes welled with tears. Although I was heartbroken, I could not cry, and that inability got me thinking and looking upward. *God, are you telling me there's no need to cry? Chloe's not gone forever?*

When I got home, I went onto Placer SPCA's website and submitted an official, detailed lost-pet report with photos. All I could really do was wait, pray, and keep the faith that Chloe knew my backyard was her official home and she'd come back. I'd have to count on God to watch over her in the meantime.

# NO PLACE LIKE HOME

If I'd have been a free-spirit rabbit, hopping around the neighborhood, lying on porches or under shrubbery, and nibbling on fescue, I can imagine how panic would arise when the only way out of a yard with six-foot high cedar fencing became blocked. I'd frantically search for an escape too, even if it meant digging my way back to freedom.

A night had already passed since Chloe left. I had placed all her favorite foods out on the deck and stayed awake as long as I could to watch for her, hoping she'd return. But the morning came and her food hadn't been touched. My mom used to come over when I was on business trips and make sure Chloe had food and water. I shared with her that Chloe hadn't come home and may never again. Mom encouraged me to stay optimistic that Chloe would be back. She said the accommodations were great at my house; why wouldn't she? My dad expressed the same sentiment.

I put fresh food out for Chloe on night two. I kept the slider open again, so I could listen for her. I even replaced my yard light with a softer yellow bulb, so I could see more clearly and yet not scare her away with a bright light.

I'd look out frequently, and about 11:00 PM something moving up the deck stairs and under the patio table caught my attention. It was Chloe. She had returned!

I rushed out to my side gate and this time, built Fort Knox with my own hands, putting every heavy item I could find against the gate and covering every possible escape route that I could see. Now, she would be safe in my backyard, a permanent home for her.

I stayed up for a while and watched Chloe eat. It brought me joy and relief. She was finally home for good. I prayed that what I had constructed in my yard would keep her in. I had hoped she wouldn't get any bright ideas and decide to dig her way to freedom along another stretch of my fence. Neighbors on all three sides had dogs, and Chloe wouldn't survive an encounter with them; and of course, there was the cruel guy on the north side who tried to trap her just days before. It would no doubt turn fatal if she went that direction.

Once daylight returned and I saw that Chloe was still home, I went out and inspected the perimeter of my fence. Since Chloe dug through dirt to get out the first time, there were stretches along the bottom of the fence that I worried she'd dig through. I pulled river rock from my landscaped backyard and put them in those areas and then headed to my home improvement store.

I found black metal fence panels in the garden section. They had a decorative design on top, making them a far from inexpensive option, but they were perfect for keeping in a wayward rabbit. The material was sturdy, portable, easy to assemble, and Chloe wouldn't be able to slip through the gaps in the wiring. I spent a small fortune just to protect my cherished Palomino bunny, but she was worth every penny.

I called my dad over because he was always great at DIY home projects. We encircled my entire yard with the black metal fence.

I wasn't satisfied that the property line between my yard and the callous neighbor to the north wouldn't be crossed. I worried that Chloe would dig through the dirt to his side. I concluded that concrete was the only sure stop. So, poor Dad. He went to work on mixing cement and digging a trench just so I could pour it along the bottom of the fence line. My dad is the best! I could tell that he enjoyed having Chloe around, especially when she'd hop up to him during our yard project.

Chloe stayed nearby, watching the evolution of her former entryway as we worked. She convinced me that she was far from pleased with her new reality. I heard a thump. Then a thump, thump. It was Chloe exhibiting her frustration with a blocked side yard. One of the reasons that rabbits stomp their feet is because they are expressing anger or annoyance. If only we could get this rabbit to understand that what we were doing was for her own good.

## LIFE OF LUXURY

It didn't take long for Chloe to settle in. She had acquired favorite places in my yard even when she used to come and go, but now she had more time to indulge in the amenities.

I'd see her lying on my deck with her hind feet stretched back. That was my favorite pose of hers. She looked so cute with her little fuzzy white tail above her exposed feet while she relaxed. I'd water the dirt in my rose garden so she could rest on cool ground underneath the rosebushes on hot days. I kept the lower part pruned so they'd be more like trees to provide shade for her.

She definitely made herself at home. She got up on top of the patio table using its matching chairs as her launch pad, and she hopped up on the wooden and cement benches in my yard and lay for hours. I couldn't believe it one day when I saw her sitting on top of my air conditioning unit compressor.

My two indoor cats would sit at the sliding door's aluminum wire screen and watch Chloe move about outdoors. She'd hop up on the deck when she'd see my cats and they'd rub noses through the screen. Chloe never came in the house. I felt it was best that she roamed free in the backyard. I didn't want to risk her chewing on electric cords and hurting herself in my house after witnessing her frustration with the tubing of my drip sprinkler system.

That system was no match for Chloe. If a drip line was in her path and she didn't like having to hop over it, she chewed a hole right through it. If she didn't like that dirt was covering the large plastic sprinkler pipe, she'd uncover it. Chloe liked things a certain way and no one was ever going to change her mind. (I can relate.)

In winter months, I leaned a plywood panel against the patio table, so she'd have protection against the elements. I lined my grandfather's old wooden box with straw hay so she could have a warm bed. I tried to keep to a set feeding schedule of produce and alfalfa pellets every morning and night. I always knew when I was late, because Chloe would hop back and forth in front of my sliding door to grab my attention.

I stumbled onto her favorite food by accident. I gave Chloe a leftover baked sweet potato from Thanksgiving dinner, and that yam disappeared faster than a Dyson vacuum cleaner suctioning the floor on its highest setting. There wasn't a crumb left when she was done. She might have expected to continue living the high life and eating baked sweet potatoes. But sometimes the cook was off duty and raw ones were all she got.

Whenever the bimonthly pest control service technician came to my home, he was extra-careful not to spray where Chloe was situated in the yard. I'd have to cut black zip-ties to open panels of the decorative metal fence so he could get in to treat both sides of my house. I'd stand there, make sure Chloe didn't follow, let him out when he was done, and then close and re-secure the panels.

Lucky for Chloe and me, our pest control guy used to have a rabbit, so he not only always made sure she was a safe distance away from pesticides, but he'd stop and pet her. Chloe would only allow one other person to pet her: me. I wish I could have held her, but I never could. Her hair was as silky as a kitten's. I loved it most when she allowed my gentle touch on the golden baby-soft fur between her ears. Her eyes would close and she wouldn't move, almost falling asleep.

She'd follow me whenever I was in the backyard. Often, she'd be right at my feet. My parents and friends also enjoyed having Chloe around in the yard. I'd take pictures of her going about her daily life or doing silly things, and I also took holiday-themed photos with Chloe as the top model. I'd share them on social media, and everyone loved it.

One time, both of my parents were helping me with a yard project. We were busy working when we were interrupted by Chloe's frantic behavior. She hastily hopped around the yard, grabbing twigs, grass, and straw, rushing under the deck and then back out. It seemed like she was building a nest. She had lived permanently in my backyard for about a year by that time, so we knew she couldn't possibly be pregnant.

When our project was done for the day, I headed for my computer. I was still perplexed at why Chloe was acting the way she was. I discovered that rabbits can have false (otherwise known as phantom or pseudo) pregnancies. She definitely acted like that was the case, because I noticed that she was also bending her neck and pulling fur from her body. That's another sign she was actively preparing the lining for her nest.

Chloe's behavior continued for another couple of days, not as long as my online search suggested might happen. Nevertheless, I learned that one of the reasons for false pregnancies was stress. Something was stressing her out, but I didn't know what it was at the time.

# MISCREANTS

The neighbors directly behind my house had two awful boys about four and six years old. They seemed always out of control. The mother was constantly screaming at them or the dog, Bruno. She even had the nerve to yell from her second-floor window to my next-door neighbors who were out in their backyard (a nice, never-cause-any-problems family) that *their* dog barked too much.

I swear her voice could be heard for miles. She used to sit in her backyard and chat on her cell phone so loud I could hear every word she said. You'd never know there was a father around. I could see his silhouette through the cracks of light between the fence boards, but I could barely hear his conversations.

I was away one afternoon and when I returned, I saw black lava rock all over my redwood deck. Chloe was lying under a shrub and I sensed she was scared. The pint-size miscreants were in their backyard with their friends, jumping up and down on a trampoline, and running around on the lawn next to their swimming pool.

It occurred to me that the whole group of troublemakers probably saw my rabbit when they jumped high enough to look over my fence, and instead of admiring an adorable bunny, they threw rocks at her.

I knew it was them. The way items fell in my backyard meant they came from that direction. Usually, I'd find plastic toys and balls in my yard (which I sometimes threw back over the fence). I came to the conclusion that they were privileged kids, because they came to my house only once and asked for their beach ball. Otherwise, it seemed they didn't even miss their stuff.

Because their mother was quite somethin', I didn't want to confront her. My nice neighbors next door had told me they never wanted to deal with her either. But I knew I needed to do something to block out those hoodlums. I couldn't risk a repeat of the meteor shower Chloe had endured.

I went to my home improvement store, yet again, and bought rolls of 6' x 6' bamboo garden fencing and a staple gun. I knew I had to act fast to create a higher wall while the entire family was at work and school. I asked my dad for help to make sure I was attaching the bamboo properly. He came over and we worked together to staple the bamboo fencing all along the back fence wall to where it would stick up about two feet higher than the wood.

Looking back, I see now how my actions were definitely cray-cray, but I was so mad at those little rascals for scaring my sweet Chloe.

The bamboo wall made my backyard look like I was a castaway living on Gilligan's Island. It held well until the following day when strong winds caused it to lean. I asked my dad for advice on how to find a better way to support the bamboo fencing attached to my cedar fence. He offered to help and I took him up on it. However, the day was drawing to a close and more than likely, the blonde-bob neighborhood loud-mouth was already home from work. I had a sinking feeling that if she saw us in my backyard, she'd have something to say.

Sure enough, as we were repairing the bamboo wall, I saw Bad Mom peering out her second-floor window and I knew she was headed our way. It took her only a minute or so to arrive at the fence line which separated our backyards to gripe about how bad my bamboo creation looked. I felt emboldened with Dad as my bodyguard and decided to tell her exactly why I did it.

I told her that her kids were throwing rocks at my rabbit. Of course, based on how *well-disciplined* her boys were, she defended them saying they'd never do that. I repeated to her that they did. I even showed her one of the rocks which I had kept in a bucket as my "evidence" of their "crime." She seemed to believe me then and said I should have just come to her door and let her know so she could have told her sons to stop. *Yeah, right* crossed my mind as I agreed to remove all traces of our two-day bamboo partition.

I learned to live with their annoying behavior and the lack of privacy from their messy blonde heads bouncing up and down over the back fence when they used their trampoline, but at least foreign lava rocks never again appeared on my redwood deck or in my backyard. My gut tells me that they may have started harassing Chloe before the lava rock downpour afternoon. They may have yelled over the fence or threw a rock or two at her, which brought on her pseudopregnancy. If the rocks were small, they would have blended in with the rock already in my landscape.

Who knows if those two brats were given a talkin' to or a time-out regarding throwing things over the fence, but I think it's safe to say that my unconventional idea got their attention. Chloe never endured another rock attack. No matter how nutty attaching bamboo to a shared fence line might sound to some, I'd do it again in a heartbeat just to protect my precious Palomino gem.

# YOU'RE ON MY TURF

It brought me great joy to see Chloe move about her bunny sanctuary. I used to love watching her from inside my house hop on each of the 16-inch aggregate stepping stones from one end of the yard to my redwood deck and up the one and only step to reach the slider and a smorgasbord of cuisine under my patio table. Sometimes she'd stop midway down the path and pause for a couple of minutes. From the side, her profile looked like a chocolate Easter bunny for sale in springtime. I swear she saw me gazing at her from inside my home.

I think Chloe looked forward to me spending time with her in the yard. She always seemed happy to see me when I entered her oasis. She'd hop up to me as if to offer a friendly "welcome to my home" greeting. Sometimes, she'd kick her hind legs up high and twist her body as she hopscotched around the yard. That clued me in to the bliss she was experiencing. There's actually a term for when a rabbit spontaneously leaps in the air and does body twists or leg kicks—binky.

Other times, she looked so comfortable lounging inside a large, black resin planter. It felt like she begrudgingly hopped out to greet me with "didn't you see my *Do Not Disturb* sign?" insinuation.

There was a corner of my lawn that was a brighter green and grew faster than any other section. I soon discovered that it had become Chloe's lavatory. She kept her sanctuary tidy, and that area was the only spot in my entire yard where she "conducted serious business."

Of course, a yard half filled with fescue needed to be mowed. I tried not to upset Chloe by mowing as quickly as I could in areas where she wasn't sitting. Even though Chloe tried to help me keep the fescue trimmed, she and I both knew that a bunny can only do so much.

She seemed to especially love when I pruned shrubs so she could help nibble up what my raking had missed. Never a dull moment with Chloe around.

It's mind-boggling for me to think of how someone could abandon a pet because they enrich our lives in so many ways. I read online that rabbits are the third most surrendered animal to rescues in the United States, after cats and dogs.

Oftentimes, rabbits are a seasonal impulse buy at Easter without any consideration for long-term care. As a native Californian, I was extremely thrilled to learn that Governor Jerry Brown had signed Assembly Bill 485 on October 13, 2017 to ban the sale of commercially bred cats, dogs, and rabbits from pet stores. The law took effect on January 1, 2019 and per the legislative counsel's digest for AB 485, all cats, dogs, and rabbits available at California pet stores would have to come from a public animal control agency or shelter, Society for the Prevention of Cruelty to Animals shelter, humane society shelter, or rescue group. Awesome news!

I'm glad I could make a difference in the life of one of those statistics before Assembly Bill 485 took effect, but that *statistic* actually made my life better by leaps and bounds.

Chloe had tons of character packed into her little body. She brought me happiness and laughter those days when I really needed an uplift. Seeing her lying on my deck with her hind feet stretched back and exposed beneath her fuzzy white tail, offered me a sense of calm when the weight of my world was too heavy to bear. I needed Chloe and she needed me, plain and simple.

## CHANGING SEASONS

Orange leaves on the maple trees confirmed that autumn had arrived. The days were becoming shorter and cooler. I went out to feed Chloe the morning of October 28, 2013, and noticed that she had not touched the alfalfa pellets, spring mix, or carrots that I had left out for her the night before. I saw her resting in the bed of my rose garden, so I knelt down and stroked her favorite spot—the baby-soft fur between her ears. Caressing mesmerized her for a few minutes and then she hopped over to drink from her water bowl. Since she was moving about, it hadn't occurred to me that something was wrong. I left for work, hoping she'd eat all her food.

But when I arrived back home, I had a sinking feeling. Her food remained untouched. I remembered that for two or three weeks, she had been going under the redwood deck which was built on concrete piers and making noises which sounded like feverish digging in the dirt and scratching against the house. When I'd step out of the slider and onto the deck, I'd hear the ruckus and see her through the gaps in the wood slats.

Perhaps it was my instincts telling me something was terribly wrong or divine prompting that caused me to look down the moment I stepped through the threshold of the screen door and out onto my redwood deck that evening, but I did. All it took was seeing a beautiful, motionless white tail to cause my heart to shatter. *No! Chloe!*

I could see her underneath the deck along the house in the middle. I called my dad for help as my despair caused me not to think clearly as to how to remove her. After Dad got to my house and assessed the situation, he unscrewed deck screws and removed two rows of deck boards. Chloe was laying completely still on the ground. She was gone. I wept as reality that God had called my sweet little girl home hit me hard. We pulled Chloe out from under the deck, wrapped her in a pale blue bath towel, placed her in a plastic container, and buried her in a sacred place amid a patch of petunias.

The following day saddened me terribly. I removed shriveled up remnants of produce and unused alfalfa pellets, tore down the makeshift plywood dwelling I had set up against the patio table, and looked out onto my quiet, gloomy backyard. It wasn't the same without Chloe there. She had been the light through some dark personal and professional days.

I ended up selling my home a year later. It took a while, but when I finally accepted Chloe's death, I reminded myself that everything happens in God's timing. I had no control over her passing. My backyard had been her home for two years and moving her to another backyard might have been too stressful, especially since she wouldn't let me or anyone else pick her up.

A bond began to form the moment Chloe appeared at my sliding door that summer day. Our time together may have been short, but it was jam-packed with adventure, joy, and mutual love. My special girl has left a permanent footprint on a heart that still aches with the loss; I miss her so much. My hope is that by sharing our story, homeless animals will be adopted in Chloe's memory and cherished every day.

It's quite remarkable that Chloe ended up choosing her final resting place to be underneath the same deck that she had hopped up on the day she adopted me. It must have been the spot where she felt most safe and at peace. I guess you could call that full circle.

## LOVE LETTER

Dearest Chloe,
There will never be another you. This I know for sure. You were one of a kind and enriched my life more than you'll ever know.

I still grieve for our friendship in physical form. I long to stroke the ultra-soft fur between your ears and watch your eyes relax in delight. When you ate the smorgasbord of cuisine that I left out for you, I couldn't help but stop and admire your darling pink nose and tiny white teeth as you nibbled. It was so cute. I miss seeing you lounging in the yard or on the deck. Your contentment warmed my heart and made me smile wide each time.

When I saw you sitting atop a garden bench, sunning on the patio table, or snuggled in the black resin planter, I couldn't help but beam and be captivated by your self-assurance and intelligence. You showed me how confidence can broaden our world. I want the carefree, do-whatever-makes-me-happy attitude that you had. You taught me the importance of having a more lighthearted take on life.

You may not have been thrilled at first when I blocked your way in and out of my backyard, but I don't think you truly knew the danger you were in living alone on the streets. You were a gift from God, and I didn't want any harm to come to you. I have regretted not having you live indoors with me, because maybe that would have prolonged your life. But I believe that the backyard sanctuary I created just for you provided as close to the freedom you once had, with protection from predators and vehicles and the promise of food, water, and shelter. You showed me every day that you found bliss there.

It will be a glorious moment to see you again in Heaven when the time comes for me to head home, my cherished Palomino angel. Our bond is eternal, and I know you'll be just as happy to see me as I will you. You will hop up to me as I kneel to stroke the baby-soft fur between your ears. It'll be just like old times.

I'll never forget the day you hopped up to my door and your brown eyes stole my heart. You will always be my valentine, as my love for you will never wane. Thank you, Chloe, for choosing me.

## ABOUT THE AUTHOR

Denise Lee Branco is an award-winning author and inspirational speaker, whose passion is using her writing to advocate for animal adoption and to mentor pet parents facing and experiencing pet loss through their grief. Denise believes that the path toward healing includes opening our heart and home to another animal awaiting adoption. She treasures memories and time spent with each pet that has graced her life, and she desires that same feeling for every person in the world.

Denise's first book, *Horse at the Corner Post: Our Divine Journey*, won a silver medal in the Living Now Book Awards in 2011. Her article, *When You Are Called Upon*, won a Cat Writers Association Certificate of Excellence in 2018. She is a member of several writing and publishing organizations and has been a contributor to twelve anthologies. She is a Certified Pet Loss Grief Specialist-Individual through the Center for Pet Loss Grief, LLC.

Her first pet rabbit, when she was a young girl, was a Silver rabbit named Cleo. Denise also raised New Zealand rabbits as a 4-H project in her youth. She now lives in the foothills of Northern California and loves leisure biking, foods with melted cheese, and spoiling her three rescued felines.

Visit www.DeniseInspiresYou.com to learn more about Denise, read her blog, purchase books, and subscribe to her newsletter for the latest happenings, book signings, and speaking events.

# ACKNOWLEDGMENTS

Special thanks to my fellow *From Plot to Print* course authors, June Gillam, Penny Clark, and Sandra Simmer, and our exceptional instructor Michelle Hamilton, for your constant encouragement and honest feedback as I developed Chloe's story. I grew as a writer because of you ladies, not only in scene development and storytelling, but by the gentle way you used humor to enlighten me of my shortfalls.

Michelle, I know that if you had not offered your first *From Plot to Print* course to members of Northern California Publishers and Authors last summer, I'd still be uncertain as to how I'd best pay tribute to Chloe. I believe everything happens according to Divine order, and this is no exception. Now, is definitely the right time.

Heartfelt appreciation to all my advance reviewers.

I'm ever so grateful that you agreed without hesitation to read my work. Your advice helped Chloe's story come to life on the pages of this book, and I'm truly honored to receive your beautiful endorsements.

I am deeply grateful to Christine Horner, The Book Cover Whisperer, who came to my rescue on short notice to design this book. She not only helped me meet a tight publication deadline, but she took my vision and created something better than I could have imagined. Thank you, Christine, for understanding my passion to honor my sweet Chloe in the best possible way.

Loving thanks to my dear parents. I will never forget how you helped me give Chloe the best rabbit sanctuary a bunny could have. Thank you from the bottom of my heart, Mom and Dad, for surrounding me with animals since the day I was born. They make my life whole.

I thank my Heavenly father for guiding Chloe on her path to me. She was the best unexpected gift I'd received since reuniting with my beloved horse, Freedom.

To everyone who knew Chloe from the beginning, or are meeting her for the first time now, thank you for the joy you've given me by your delight in her. My purpose in life is to better the lives of animals, and I couldn't do that without your support.

Most of all, to abandoned bunnies all over the world. May this year be the year a divine path leads you to your forever home. I promise to do all I can in Chloe's memory to help make that wish come true. My little Palomino gem had a gleaming life purpose from the moment she arrived at my sliding door, and it's now shining brighter than ever.

*Much Love,*
*Denise*

# RESOURCES

Placer SPCA, 200 Tahoe Avenue, Roseville, CA 95678 & 1482 Grass Valley Highway, Auburn, CA 95603. Visit https://www.placerspca.org

House Rabbit Society, 148 Broadway, Richmond, CA 94804. Visit https://rabbit.org/ (A $20 donation gets you a one-year membership to HRS, which includes several discounts to online rabbit toy and supply shops and their bi-annual magazine, the *House Rabbit Journal*.)

Cannon Beach Bunny Rescue, 4230 SE King Road #183, Milwaukie, OR 97222. Visit https://www. cannonbeachbunnyrescue.org

Bunny Bunch Rabbit Rescue, visit bunnybunch. org & bunnybunchboutique.com, at 4601-1 Brooks Street, Montclair, CA 91763 & 10534 Bechler River Avenue, Fountain Valley, CA 92708. (Watch *Caroline and the Bunnies* - Rabbit Care, Health, & Lifestyle on YouTube.)

Friends of Unwanted Rabbits (FUR), P. O. Box 882, Folsom, CA 95763. Visit http://www.friendsofunwantedrabbits.org

Center for Pet Loss Grief, LLC, visit https://www.centerforpetlossgrief.com

California Legislature, search AB 485 (2017-2018) at https://www.leginfo.legislature.ca.gov

*Please remember to support your local animal rescues.*

*THANK YOU*
*for Reading*

*Rabbit at the Sliding Door:*
*Chloe's Story*

Hɪ, ᴍʏ ɴᴀᴍᴇ ɪs Cʜʟᴏᴇ, writing to you from beautiful Heaven. Thank you for reading my story. Since this book is dedicated to me and all abandoned bunnies, it would mean so much if you left a review on Amazon, Barnes & Noble, Goodreads, or wherever you choose. A portion of sales will be donated to animal rescue organizations. So, the more books purchased, the more animals we can help.

Thanks again for making a difference in the lives of animals all over the world.

CPSIA information can be obtained
at www.ICGtesting.com
Printed in the USA
LVHW072047190322
713895LV00001B/1